MY COMFORTERS

My mouth praises thee with joyful lips,

When I think of thee upon my bed,

And meditate on thee in the watches of the night;

For thou hast been my help,

And in the shadow of thy wings I sing for joy.

—Psalm 63:5b-7

MY COMFORTERS

A Book of Daily Inspiration for Those Who Are Ill

By Helen Good Brenneman

HERALD PRESS, SCOTTDALE, PENNSYLVANIA
KITCHENER, ONTARIO

MY COMFORTERS

Copyright © 1966 by Herald Press, Scottdale, Pa. 15683
Library of Congress Catalog Card Number: 66-13156
International Standard Book Numbers:
  0-8361-1751-4 (hardcover)
  0-8361-1529-5 (softcover)
Printed in the United States of America
Third Printing, 1974

To My Own Comforters—
Virgil, Don
Lois Ann
John Michael
and
Rebecca
This book is lovingly dedicated.

Preface

This little volume is a sharing—a sharing of inspiration and love passed on to me by friends in an hour of deepest need. For I have just come home from a month at the hospital, and although I am not cured, God has answered many of the prayers of my friends. My friends have given generously of their love and encouragement. Now, I, like the Apostle Paul, would "comfort them which are in any trouble, by the comfort wherewith [I myself am] comforted of God."

My hospital experiences in years gone by were of two varieties—a tonsillectomy at an early age and four maternity stays, each with an ecstatic joy and a baby to show for the trouble. But this was different. I had known for a year that I was a victim of multiple sclerosis, but had hoped that mine would continue to be a light case. When, suddenly, I became more and more disabled within the period of two weeks, I panicked. How frightening to go to bed at night, not knowing if one could get up in the morning! A fear of helplessness overwhelmed me as I found myself leaning heavily on the arm of my husband, or as I fell just walking across the dining-room floor! A few days after hospitalization I had no use of my legs, and I discovered that my right hand was spastic, my left hand partially disabled.

Now I lived in a foreign land—one as unfamiliar as Cambodia or a South Sea island. The world of efficient but overtaxed nurses, stretchers, IV injections, tests of every kind, spinal taps, blood pressures, thermometers was mine, and what discomfort I was spared at the moment, one of my roommates was usually undergoing. And, in my weakness, I found it difficult to handle the problem of suffering—not only my own, but the pain of neighbors who were far worse off than I.

Multiple sclerosis is an incurable disease of the central nervous system, which leaves its victims in varying degrees of disability. Most frustrating is its uncertainty. Not even the doctors can assure one of what it will do tomorrow or what new symptoms may appear. In fact, doctors are careful to be noncommittal, never to offer false hope to the patient.

It was at a dark moment that a young doctor came to my bedside. "You won't be seeing me again," he informed me, "as I am being transferred to another department." I poured out some of my doubts and fears. He looked at me a bit severely, though there was kindness in his voice. "But you have resources," he said, "resources that so many in this hospital do not have."

I was to think of these words many times in the days that followed. For I had the prayer support of numerous congregations, and day after day letters from praying friends came in a steady stream, to be read and reread. There were flowers, too—from a prayer group back home, from a Sunday-school class, from relatives and acquaintances, fresh-growing symbols of love and support. And there were those who presented themselves in person for a chat and a warm touch of the hand. Sick I was, and they visited me.

Across from me lay one who had only one relative, in a distant state. She had had a dog, but he had been in a kennel for three months, and could hardly visit her. She had one friend, who did come once for a visit. Mail? None. Flowers? Only those I shared with her. Prayer? How grateful she was when my minister-father prayed with her!

Resources? Yes, they were mine—Christian brotherhood, expressed to me and to my husband and four children at home. Love poured out. Prayer rising as incense from many altars. But, best of all, there was the continual, living presence of Christ Himself, mine to share with those around me.

Every card received in the hospital is a reminder that someone cares. But I could not help noticing the superficiality of some greetings which fellow patients received. "Operations are like corsets," one greeting read, though I don't remember just how the idea was further developed. But I do know that operations are not a joke to those who face them. How much more helpful are the words of the Twenty-third Psalm, "Yea, though I walk through the valley of the shadow of death, I will fear no evil: for thou art with me."

I often had to think of poor Job and his "miserable comforters," as I depended upon the loving support of friends. As I said in the beginning of this preface, God answered prayer in a marvelous way. I was to walk again and to regain the use of my hands, though with limitations and handicap.

The author wishes to gratefully acknowledge permission to

quote from various books as noted in the footnotes. In addition she appreciated the help received from *Halley's Bible Handbook* by Henry H. Halley and *How God Heals* by Paul M. Miller. I would like to thank Evelyn Bauer for sharing her "poem-friends" with me, some of which were used in this book.

The following pages were inspired largely by cards and letters which came to me from those who cared, words which helped me lift my eyes to God. Visit, if you will, with my friends, my "memorable comforters."

First Day

"Now Mine Eye Seeth Thee"

When we are well, racing through our days to accomplish our many tasks, caring for our families, meeting with our committees, hoeing the weeds in our gardens, it is easy to forget our friends who are temporarily, or even permanently, on the shelf. It is only when we ourselves lie on a so-called "bed of affliction," that we fully realize the importance of human comfort, particularly in the form of flesh-and-blood friends. In a hospital, one even begins to look forward to his roommate's visitors!

Of all those who came to visit me or sent letters of prayerful concern not one could be called a "miserable comforter." But long ago, in the land of Uz, there lived a man whose friends failed him in the crisis of his life. Job had been a particularly fortunate person, bringing up a fine family of ten children, farming a fertile land, and owning vast herds of oxen, sheep, and camels. He was a chieftain, a desert prince, a man of wealth, influence, and integrity. That is, he was all these things until God allowed Satan to try him, to see if suffering would cause him to lose his faith in God.

Satan, who had been "going to and fro in the earth, and . . . walking up and down in it," making a nuisance of himself, came to God and accused Job of serving Him simply because God prospered him. To make a long story short, God allowed Satan to bring great trouble to Job. In a series of disasters (theft, murder, a thunderstorm, and a cyclone), Job lost all his worldly possessions and his family, with the exception of his wife. And then God allowed Job to be smitten with leprosy.

Probably Job's most miserable comforter was the person who should have been his greatest comfort—his wife. Her words: "Why don't you curse God, and die?" Fortunately, Job didn't take her advice, but he did become greatly depressed. In a deep sob of anguish, he cried, "Oh, if I had only never been born!"

Three friends came to visit Job, and they didn't follow the hospital etiquette of short visits. At first, they sat down beside him for seven days and seven nights, just sharing his grief. This period of silence was the wisest part of their visit. It was when they opened their mouths to "comfort" Job, they got into trouble.

In long speeches aimed at their ailing friend, Bildad, Zophar, and Eliphaz scolded Job for being a hypocrite, explaining carefully to him that suffering is a punishment for sin. By intimation and direct accusation, they suggested some of the specific sins of which Job had probably been guilty. Another friend, Elihu, waited until the older men were finished and then added his less cruel advice that God was disciplining Job.

Out of a whirlwind God asks Job one question after another, showing him His own greatness and Job's helplessness and smallness compared to God. Job is sorry that he doubted God's love and repents of his lack of faith. God also reproves Job's so-called friends, who were all wrong in their idea that Job was suffering for his sins. Job, instead, was being tried. As he had said himself "When he hath tried me, I shall come forth as gold."

God rewarded Job for his integrity, blessing him with ten more children, renewed health and strength, and even greater wealth than he had known in his younger years. But the greatest reward for Job—and for us, who, too, may suffer, was that through his suffering Job came to know God in a deeper and more intimate way. He said, "I have heard of thee by the hearing of the ear: but now mine eye seeth thee."

Why do the innocent suffer? This problem is not really solved in the Book of Job, and is just as much a puzzle to us in our day. But we do know that God Himself understands when we suffer, for He partook of human suffering in the person of His Son, Jesus Christ. Someday, in His presence, we will understand.

Word of Comfort:

> For I am convinced that there is nothing
>   in death or life,
> in the realm of spirits or superhuman powers,
> in the world as it is or the world as it shall be,
> in the forces of the universe, in heights or depths—
> nothing in all creation that can separate us
>   from the love of God in Christ Jesus our Lord.
>   —Romans 8:38, 39, NEB[1]

1. From the *New English Bible.* © The Delegates of the Oxford University Press and the Syndics of the Cambridge University Press, 1961. Used by permission. Other quotations from this Bible are indicated by "NEB."

Second Day

My Life . . . in His Hands

This letter is postmarked from our hometown in Indiana, which we left this year for a period of schooling. Little did we know, when we left, what special lessons God had for us in His own classroom! But, back to the letter. I feel a twinge of nostalgia when I read this letter, for it comes from one of our near neighbors, and thoughts of her take me right into my own kitchen. It is a large, ample farm kitchen, and Doris is seated across the table, sharing a cup of coffee and Christian fellowship that is real.

"Helen," my good neighbor begins, "it's just a little more than a year ago since I shared my wonderful experience with you, and you listened so graciously while I was endeavoring to understand just what it all meant. I have learned and am still learning to walk with God step by step and am sure it is the same with you. Romans 11:33 has always been a favorite verse of mine and now more than ever: 'O the depth of the riches both of the wisdom and knowledge of God! how unsearchable are his judgments, and his ways past finding out!' "

God has no stereotyped ways with His children. One night, in the middle of the quiet hours, He surrounded my friend with His loving presence in a real and new way. How inspiring it was to have her share this dynamic experience with me! How our fellowship deepened as we talked together of the Lord—just snatches on the telephone or over a cup of coffee!

And now God is speaking to me in a new and different way, not in a call in the night, but in His still, small voice. He has asked me to be still and know that He is God. He has asked me to trust Him in a difficult experience.

But Doris's letter is not finished. She writes, "Here is my paraphrasing of the Twenty-third Psalm. I thought you, too, might find rest in it." (And I did!)

"My life is in God's hands.

I am satisfied!

He gives me rest and peace.
His hand leads me all the way.
If I fall, He lifts me up.
He leads me in paths that are right and good
    for His honor and glory.
Even though things look dark and I cannot feel
    His presence, yet by faith I know that He
    is with me and surrounding me.
He will give me all the resources I need,
    even though circumstances seem to be working
    against me.
He gives me joy so abundant that it overflows,
His loving, guiding hand shall lead me throughout life
    until I am in His presence forevermore."

Word of Comfort:

The Lord is my shepherd; I shall not want.
He maketh me to lie down in green pastures:
he leadeth me beside the still waters.
He restoreth my soul:
he leadeth me in the paths of righteousness for his name's sake.
Yea, though I walk through the valley of the shadow of death,
    I will fear no evil: for thou art with me;
thy rod and thy staff they comfort me.
Thou preparest a table before me in the presence
of mine enemies:
thou anointest my head with oil; my cup runneth over.
Surely goodness and mercy shall follow me all the days of my life,
    and I shall dwell in the house of the Lord for ever.

                                                     —Psalm 23

Third Day

God's Compensations

It is winter as I write this, and a letter comes from a dear friend in Indiana, where winters can be both confining and calendar-like in their beauty. It's not hard to imagine Evelyn's scene from her picture window. She writes, "Last week one day we had the most beautiful hoarfrost—the kind that doesn't happen every year. A sight like that helps make up for the cold and inconvenience of winter! This also reminds me of the compensations God sends us in our more difficult situations. I know you are experiencing this, too. Truly God is good."

Evelyn should and does know about those compensations. In 1953 she and her husband, Royal Bauer, were unexpectedly returned to America from their chosen calling—as missionaries to India. A difficult situation? Yes. For Evelyn had bulbar polio, which almost took her life and confined her to a wheelchair for the rest of her days. From this experience, Evelyn wrote a book, *Through Sunlight and Shadow.*[1] She tells of the early days as "green" missionaries on a new field, the adjustments of learning a new language and a new culture, the joy of sharing Christ when they at last were able to communicate with their Indian friends. But, before they were really started in their ministry, Evelyn found herself in a hospital at Vellore, India, passing through the valley of the shadow of death, paralyzed in both arms and legs.

The lessons which God had for Evelyn after this experience were more difficult than the intricacies of the Hindi language. However, God's love was real to her, even during the times of intense pain. Although she thought that she would eventually walk again, her prayer was, "Thy will be done." Knowing that God's mind was greater than her own, Evelyn trusted her life unreservedly to her heavenly Father.

As I mused over the possibilities, known only to God, of facing life with handicaps similar to Evelyn's, I wondered briefly of what value I would be if I could no longer perform the duties which I felt God had called me to do. It was comforting when my husband said, "But you will still be *you.* You will still have your personhood. You will still be here to lend your influence to the rest of the family."

Evelyn, too, had learned the lesson of "being" as well as "doing." One time she signed a letter to me, "With appreciation for what you *are*." In a contribution to a book on stewardship for women, *A Farthing in Her Hand*,[2] she says,

"When an accident or some other calamity strikes one in the bloom of health very suddenly and with finality, the adjustment may be more difficult than when conditions come on gradually. Primarily, a change in objective may be necessary, a shift from an emphasis on what one *does,* to what one *is*. Our modern world places too much importance on doing rather than being. When we can no longer do as we did before, we feel useless. Phillips Brooks said, 'You ask what you can do? You can furnish one Christian life!' "

Life, Evelyn says, is an elaborate smorgasbord, of which no one can partake of all. "Yet each dish is so good that if one can have only a few, he is well rewarded. God has made life great enough, that even if one cannot have it all, he can make what he does have a priceless possession."

And that is what my friend Evelyn has done. Her life speaks to me and to many others as she writes letters to missionaries and other friends in foreign lands, as she teaches art in a Christian high school, as she writes for Christian publications (with the aid of a sling and an electric typewriter), as she paints oil canvasses for her friends, as she meets the deeper needs of her husband and son. Evelyn has tasted God's compensations. She has tasted and found that the Lord is good!

Word of Comfort:

I am come that they might have life,
and that they might have it more abundantly.
— John 10:10b

1. Evelyn Bauer, *Through Sunlight and Shadow*. Herald Press, Scottdale, Pa. 1959.
2. Helen Alderfer, Editor, *A Farthing in Her Hand*. Herald Press, Scottdale, Pa. 1964.

Fourth Day

"Help Thou Mine Unbelief!"

In my mail came several get-well cards with a tiny, enclosed mustard seed. And printed on these cards was the verse, "If ye have faith as a grain of mustard seed . . . nothing shall be impossible unto you." As I examine this seed, smaller than the head of a pin, I think of Jesus' words about the mustard seed in another place—how, though it is the tiniest of seeds, its plant grows larger than all other herbs in the garden, even sheltering birds in its branches.

But this morning I am not sure if I have even that much faith. I am like the disciples to whom Jesus often said, "O ye of little faith." I remind myself of Peter, the time he tried walking on the sea. Remember, the disciples had gone ahead in their boat, while Jesus remained behind to pray. But the Bible tells us that the wind was contrary and that the disciples were having a rough time. Suddenly they saw a ghost! After Jesus identified Himself to them, Peter wanted to try walking on the water, too. The rest of the story goes like this:

"Peter called to him: 'Lord, if it is you, tell me to come to you over the water.' 'Come,' said Jesus. Peter stepped down from the boat, and walked over the water towards Jesus. But when he saw the strength of the gale he was seized with fear; and beginning to sink, he cried, 'Save me, Lord.' Jesus at once reached out and caught hold of him, and said, 'Why did you hesitate? How little faith you have!' They then climbed into the boat; and the wind dropped. And the men in the boat fell at his feet, exclaiming, 'Truly you are the Son of God,' " (Matthew 14:28-33, NEB).

Panic, fear, doubt, worry, what negative bedfellows sometimes crawl under the covers to keep company with the sick! But the Bible tells us of persons who came to Jesus in their extremity and who were rewarded because of their faith. Jesus would say, to the sinful woman, the blind beggar, the woman with an issue of blood, the thankful leper, "Thy faith hath saved thee. . . . Thy faith hath made thee whole." To one woman, a Canaanite, He said, "Great is thy faith."

What was the difference between those whom Jesus commended and those whom He reproved? Perhaps it was a simple remembrance of the presence of Christ in their situation and of His overcoming wisdom and power. On occasions where faith was weak, such as Peter's experience, panic took over when Peter forgot that Christ was there.

One man, in coming to Jesus with his epileptic son, confessed to his lack of faith. With tears he cried, "Lord, I believe; help thou mine unbelief." And the disciples, realizing their own need for more faith, begged, "Lord, increase our faith." It was then that Jesus answered them, "If ye had faith as a grain of mustard seed, ye might say unto this sycamine tree, Be thou plucked up by the root, and be thou planted in the sea; and it should obey you."

Barbara Shenk, a mother of a large family, who had to be separated from her children during a recent illness, wrote these lines:

Some saints must watch at the window
While others can harrow and hoe.
In their hearts they cultivate mustard,
For its seed can move mountains they know.

The *Amplified New Testament* explains faith as, "the leaning of your entire human personality on Him in absolute trust and confidence in His power, wisdom and goodness." Let us pray that we may trust, lean our entire personalities on Him, confident of His love for us. Let us ask Him to increase our faith.

Word of Comfort:

And, lo, I am with you alway, even unto the
end of the world. Amen.

—Matthew 28:20b

Fifth Day

Special with Him

When I saw the return address on the envelope, I opened the letter eagerly, knowing that there would be some brief but meaningful gem of wisdom therein. For all notes from Christine reflect the depth of her Christian living. A former missionary to China, Christine lives a quiet and thoughtful life, sharing herself with her international friends on whatever campus she happens to be teaching at the time. Since her home is usually a small apartment, tastefully furnished with Oriental decor, she seats her guests on the rug. Then she pours them some delightfully pungent tea, or allows them to cook a native meal in her little kitchen.

I used to think that whenever I visited with Christine, it was as though she dipped down into a deep well of spiritual insight and brought up something especially helpful to me. Others must feel the same way, for wherever she is, there is a continual padding of feet to her doorway, as she shares what the Holy Spirit has been saying to her.

And so I eagerly read what she has written to me on this occasion, wishing that I could visit with her face-to-face. "There have been only a few days since you are in the hospital, that I have not asked our heavenly Father to make you His very special child—during these weeks. I like to think (and I know it is true) that right now you are *special* with Him and that you feel this specialness in the same way I used to feel my parents' concern when I was sick as a child."

"Special with Him." But I am only one patient in a hospital of 1,000 beds! And, as He looks down upon the world, God cannot turn His loving eyes away from the thousands, yes, millions, of other sufferers, including those who will never enjoy the luxury of clean sheets and medical care. Yet, as another friend writes, "God is good! He knows each of us personally and treats each of us as an individual. . . . He holds you in His power and cares for you. Somehow this has been revealed to me in a new way as I think in awe of His greatness and love for each person individually—His care for *each one*."

22

The truth that God, the great God above all worlds, can care about my smallest concern, knows my temperature before the nurse takes it, knows my need before I ask it, this is beyond understanding! The Negro spiritual puts it this way:

"He's got the whole world in His hand. . . .
He's got you and me, brother, in His hand. . . ."

And a more dignified hymn, "Eternal Father," by Hervey D. Ganse, says,

Eternal Father, when to Thee,
Beyond all worlds, by faith I soar,
Before Thy boundless majesty
I stand in silence, and adore.

"But, Saviour, Thou art by my side;
Thy voice I hear, Thy face I see:
Thou art my Friend, my daily Guide;
God over all, yet God with me."

Word of Comfort:

Casting all your care upon him;
for he careth for you.

—I Peter 5:7

Sixth Day

Don't Worry!

Most frequently heard advice given at a sick bed: "Now don't you worry about a thing!"

William M. Elliott, Jr., in a book entitled, *The Cure for Anxiety*,[1] says that the word *worry* literally means "to strangle." And we have all heard how worry can kill a person. One author amusingly puts this truth in a little poem:

> One wept all night beside a sick man's bed;
> At dawn the sick was well, the mourner dead.

We know this. We appreciate the good advice of our well-meaning friends, that we shouldn't worry about a thing! We know worry may slow down our recovery. But how can we rid ourselves of the little anxieties which present themselves in such sharp focus, as we lie, day in and day out, with little else to do but to think of our troubles?

A mother, temporarily incapacitated or separated from her family, doesn't need a fertile imagination to supply her with some excellent worry material. While I lay in the hospital, my younger son had taken on a first paper route. One day he had a little accident, colliding on his bicycle with another boy. An argument resulted, ending in a threat by the opponent. This little episode did not exactly set my mind at ease!

Besides concern for our families and our own health, illness brings financial crises for most of us. An innocent-looking pill can be dreadfully expensive these days! And a doctor's call, and the cost of a hospital room!

However, this meditation was not meant to depress, but to help. In *The Cure for Anxiety*, Mr. Elliott points out that sometimes worry can be banished by action. Obviously, we cannot go out and earn our hospital bill while we are ill. We cannot get up and do our ordinary work. But there may be some things we can take action upon, such as writing a letter to get something off our mind, or talking over a problem with a trusted counselor.

And you probably guessed the other cure, prayer! Prayerful trust is God's remedy for mental and spiritual distress. A friend, hearing of my illness, wrote out the words of the Apostle Paul, as given in the Phillips' translation:

"Don't worry over anything whatever [that's pretty inclusive];
   tell God *every detail* of your needs in earnest and
      thankful prayer,
   and the peace of God, which transcends human understanding,
      will keep constant guard over your hearts and minds
   as they rest in Christ Jesus"
                              (Philippians 4:6, 7, Phillips).[2]

The italics were supplied by my friend, who has tested this verse and finds that it works.

As I lay ill, I tried this worry-remedy with every anxiety which presented itself before my imagination. Since I could not run my household, I turned it over to my husband and God. Since I could not go along on my son's paper route, I turned his safety over to his guardian angel. Since I could not go to an office and earn the hospital bill, I turned that over to God. And do you know, He did a much better job of handling all three concerns than I could have done myself!

Word of Comfort:

Cast thy burden upon the Lord,
and he shall sustain thee.

—Psalm 55:22

1. William M. Elliott, Jr., *The Cure for Anxiety.* John Knox Press, Richmond, Va. 1964.
2. From *The New Testament in Modern English,* © J. B. Phillips, 1958. Used by permission of the Macmillan Company and Geoffrey Bles, Ltd. Other quotations from this source are indicated by "Phillips."

Seventh Day

Stick in the Shovel!

The letter was signed, "Old John himself," and could have come from only one John, my brother-in-law. I had to smile at the humorous card which enclosed the letter. And, as always, John's letter also brought its smile, though sometimes one must mix tears with smiles when talking to that six-footer.

John's letter began, "You have been on my mind very much lately. I remember yet when the boys had polio. I felt you did much praying in their behalf. This is just what we are doing for you."

No, John, we will never forget those days, either. You and your plucky wife faced your ordeal with so much courage that you made the rest of us almost ashamed. Three boys in two hospitals at the same time, all seriously ill with polio. You and Mildred made the twelve-mile trip daily and managed to smile in spite of your anxiety.

You reminded me so much of Job those days, although I read nothing in the Book of Job to hint of any of the humor with which you took some of your setbacks. There was the night when, returning from the hospital, your car struck a heifer along the highway, damaging your automobile and making it necessary for you to go through a great deal of red tape to find the owner. And then, the next day, as you parked to check on your insurance, you were presented with a parking ticket. Your recital of these events supplied a light touch, which we all needed, though we sympathized with your loss. And then, to top it all, your pigs came down with some pig's disease! That seemed the last straw. Yet God saw you through your troubles. And you did your part, too.

As I lie in the hospital bed, I have to chuckle at your next paragraph. "I remember when the boys were sick, and things didn't go well financially, I tossed and couldn't sleep at night. I then decided that this would get me nowhere. I then decided to stick the shovel into whatever comes and start slinging, and it worked." How right you are, John! There are times when we must pray the prayer of helplessness, when there is nothing which we can do for ourselves. But there are other times when God expects us to stick in the shovel and start slinging. The slinging itself becomes a therapy for our souls.

And John ends on a trustful note: "I just read lately, if you don't trust, it is a form of atheism. So just trust and not worry. It isn't the wheel's turning that wears it out, it's the friction."

Oh, Lord, spare me the friction which wears out my wheels and makes it impossible for your healing hand to restore strength to my body and soul. Help me to do my part by cooperating with the doctors and nurses and by keeping my spirits up. For Jesus' sake.

Word of Comfort:

God is our refuge and strength,
a very present help in trouble.
Therefore we will not fear. . . .

—Psalm 46:1, 2a

Eighth Day

Common Things—Well Done?

Her letter was filled with concern for her friends, a minister who was ill, her neighbors, myself. "How I wish I could help you with the work and all. . . ." And I could imagine her doing just that, this saintly woman with her starchy, gingham dress. For she had always been a spiritual mother to me.

In my mind's eye I picture Blanche as I last saw her, waving us on our journey homeward after entertaining us with a good, home-cooked meal. She had remembered what we liked most, even though we hadn't eaten at her table for years. I can still smell her homemade bread and rolls. The children remember yet where she kept her cooky jar and her toy box. Those of us who were fortunate to be taken under her maternal wings know yet from whence came her wisdom and strength. The big, black Bible still holds a prominent place in her living room.

Along with Blanche's get-well card, she enclosed a newsy letter and a love gift for our family. But before our thank-you note was in the mail, another letter came from her community. It said, "Today my best friend passed away." We could scarcely believe the news that followed. Quietly and suddenly, Blanche had gone to be with her God.

There were other letters about Blanche's death, telling especially how she was missed by all generations in her church, for she had always taken time for young and old alike. Preaching the sermon at her funeral, her minister-son-in-law made a significant statement. "She did the *common* things of life *uncommonly* well."

I thought of her special ministry, which was made up entirely of common things—a gift of a loaf of bread, a dinner invitation to a discouraged widow, a friendship with a foreign student, a basket of mended clothes for a busy young pastor's wife. All done uncommonly well.

Two weeks before she died, Blanche had written to us, "These trying times come to all of us, and we dare not ask the question, Why? For God always has a purpose in all of these things. . . . We shall continue to pray that the Lord's will may be done in your life and for the good of God's people."

Why? Why was I lying in a hospital when my family needed me at home? Why had Blanche suddenly been taken when so many of us depended on her strength and cheerfulness and her love? She would not have asked, Why? Long ago she had placed her life in God's hands. Long ago she had said, "Thy will be done." Long ago she had commended her spirit to an all-knowing, all-loving Father. And this Father God is mine and yours as well.

Word of Comfort:

The eternal God is thy refuge,
and underneath are the everlasting arms.
—Deuteronomy 33:27a

Ninth Day

Friends . . . Memories

I felt as though I had walked right into her kitchen, and had had a brief sharing of her dry witticisms and her good, solid philosophies of everyday living. For, although Marie preached me no sermons, she shared herself in her brief note.

"M——— was here for lunch today, and we discussed everything from politics to cats. She knows more about politics than I do about cats [and that must be quite a bit, for Marie has quite a collection of feline friends]." Marie goes on: "When it comes to mice, she can love them a lot more than I. We have five in captivity in the living room and are thriving beyond my hopes. The boys caught eight in August, and five are still with us. I do wish they would *expire!*"

Remembering Marie's antipathy for some of the pets her sons collect, I had to admire her long-suffering in allowing these to live this long. And I thank God, as I read her letter, for friends who take time to write letters, telling the little folksy events of their days. Another friend writes, "Our days and evenings are full as usual, but I am reminded so many times that one must stop and take time to do those things we say we don't have time for."

And there are the friends who take time to stir up our remembrances. "Maybe you do not remember, but—" they begin, recalling a time of fellowship and fun.

Then I think of Glenola, with whom I have enjoyed many a delightful visit, while our children raced through the house, explored the barn, or organized exciting games on the lawn. Her Hallmark card had special meaning, therefore, because of my memories:

> Once a day, and sometimes more,
> You knock upon my daydream door,
> And I say warmly, "Come right in,
> I'm glad you're here with me again!"
> Then we sit down and have a chat,
> Recalling this, discussing that,

Until some task that I must do
Forces me away from you—

Reluctantly I say good-bye,
Smiling with a little sigh,
For though my daydreams bring you near
I wish that you were really here—
But what reality can't change
My dreams and wishes can arrange—
And through my wishing you'll be brought
To me each day, a guest in thought.

Here is a good spiritual exercise for the day: Think of a close
friend with whom you have had good times. Take an imaginary
trip into his or her home, thanking God for friendship. Then
think of the Friend who sticks closer than a brother.

Word of Comfort:

What a friend we have in Jesus,
All our sins and griefs to bear;
What a privilege to carry
Ev'rything to God in prayer!
O what peace we often forfeit,
O what needless pain we bear,
All because we do not carry
Ev'rything to God in prayer.

> —"What a Friend We Have in Jesus,"
> by Joseph Scriven

Tenth Day

"Hitherto Hath the Lord. . . ."

"As he [Jesus] was entering a village he was met by ten men with leprosy. They stood some way off and called out to him, 'Jesus, Master, take pity on us.' When he saw them he said, 'Go and show yourselves to the priests'; and while they were on their way, they were made clean. One of them, finding himself cured, turned back praising God aloud. He threw himself down at Jesus' feet and thanked him. And he was a Samaritan. At this Jesus said, 'Were not all ten cleansed? The other nine, where are they? Could none be found to come back and give praise to God except this foreigner?' And he said to the man, 'Stand up and go on your way; your faith has cured you'" (Luke 17:12-19, NEB).

A friend writes, "May we be always as quick to give thanks as to offer our petitions!" Oh, but we aren't, are we? We ask God for help, but often we are like the nine ungrateful lepers. So eager are we to enjoy the blessings of God's favor, that we forget Him who bestowed those blessings upon us.

Perhaps we feel that lying in bed with all the discomforts and insecurities of an illness, there is little to be thankful for. In this case, we need to remember the word *Ebenezer*, found in I Samuel, which means, "Hitherto hath the Lord helped us."

Close your eyes and take a series of little journeys. First of all, remember the home of your childhood. Walk, in your imagination, through each room, pausing for the happy memories which took place in this home. Thank God for the good things which happened to you as a child, the love which you knew.

Now close your eyes again, and remember a highlight of your youth. Remember a friend who influenced you toward the good and the noble, a schoolteacher, perhaps, a minister or other church worker. Thank God for His guiding hand through this stage of your life.

Next, take a mental journey to the most scenic spot you can think of—the kind of natural beauty that would make a good oil painting—a picnic spot, or the scene of a hike or a trip with your family. It may be a mountain, or a woodland in fall splendor, or a park or a river site. Refresh yourself in that memory and thank God for His creation.

Finally, think of someone whom you love. Pray God's blessing upon this friend, and thank God for friendship. Thank Him for love, the love of friends and His own love, ever present and unfailing in good times and bad.

In closing, read this verse once more from Philippians: "Don't worry over anything whatever; tell God every detail of your needs in earnest and *thankful* prayer, and the peace of God, which transcends human understanding, will keep constant guard over your hearts and minds as they rest in Christ Jesus" (Phillips).

Remind yourself of God's leading in your life up to this point (hitherto hath the Lord helped *me*). Think of His loving provisions of your needs right now, and thank Him for these things. Then, along with your thanksgiving, talk over with Him your present needs. And now, accept His peace.

Word of Comfort:

I will bless the Lord at all times:
his praise shall continually be in my mouth.

—Psalm 34:1

Eleventh Day

We'll Walk Your Road . . .

Her note was like herself, pithy and to the point. She began, "Today I had the seventh- and eighth-grade girls in Sunday school, and we were discussing you after K——— had mentioned you in our opening prayer. And with great assurance I found myself telling the girls that the turn your life has taken would not find you unprepared, but just taking a new road. You see, we were talking about patterns for happiness, and we saw anew that happiness is of the spirit, and that the joy of the Lord takes many shapes. I guess this note is just to tell you . . . that your . . . friends are walking with you as best they can down your new road."

I had to think of the roads in Dorothy's own life. Some were enchanting and exotic, some were scarcely worthy of the name. There were unexpected detours and in one case, at least, the road seemed to lead to a dead end.

In the year 1947 Dorothy and Don McCammon followed a path of divine guidance into China. During the next four years they followed China's roads by ricksha, by foot, by bus, and by jeep. These journeys, according to Dorothy's description in her book, *We Tried to Stay*,[1] were beset by "roving bandits, narrow roads not meant for vehicles, springless rickshas already occupied by some of China's millions, slippery footpaths, swinging bridges, flash floods, no service stations, brakeless buses sailing downhill with the motor off to save gas, trucks so covered with . . . extra passengers . . . that the driver can scarcely see out, roads blocked by heavy trailer loads being pushed or pulled by straining coolies. . . ."

China's paths had never been smooth! But the road became even more treacherous when the McCammons and several other missionaries tried to stay and minister to the church of China, despite the coming of the communist regime. One day Don was suddenly hauled off to prison, leaving his wife alone with the other missionary women. After a mock trial, in which the crowd of soldiers shouted for Don's assassination, he was suddenly sent out of China under guard, again leaving his pregnant wife behind.

But God was not far away, and at that very moment Don's home church, knowing nothing of the episode, was praying for him. After his departure, Baby Julie arrived safely, and after numerous trials the lady missionaries were permitted to return to America.

Don and Dorothy's next road led to Japan, where they completed another term of missionary service. But this road, too, made an unexpected detour. For their youngest child suddenly became ill and died. Mike, whose happy personality had charmed their Japanese neighbors, left behind him many friends, who also observed how God upholds His own, even in times of grief.

Dorothy's present road leads her to many parts of the United States and Canada, where she inspires groups of Christian women in their faith and service for Christ. Her wry sense of humor and vital faith are assets in letting her friends know that she, as best she can, is walking with them down their more difficult roads.

The Bible, as well as other literature, often refers to life as a pathway or road. In the Old Testament we read, "In all thy ways acknowledge him, and he shall direct thy *paths*," or, "He leadeth me in the *paths* of righteousness," or, "Show me thy ways, O Lord; teach me thy *paths*."

Mary Gardner Brainard has written a few lines about "Faith and Sight"[2] which express our feelings about the turns in the road ahead:

So I go on, not knowing,
　—I would not, if I might—
I would rather walk in the dark with God
　Than go alone in the light;
I would rather walk with Him by faith
　Than walk alone by sight.

Word of Comfort:

He knows the way that I take;
when he has tried me, I shall come forth as gold.

　　　　　　　　　　　　　　　　　　—Job 23:10

1. Dorothy S. McCammon, *We Tried to Stay.* Herald Press, Scottdale, Pa. 1953.
2. James Dalton Morrison, Editor, *Masterpieces of Religious Verse.* Harper & Brothers, New York. 1948. P. 384.

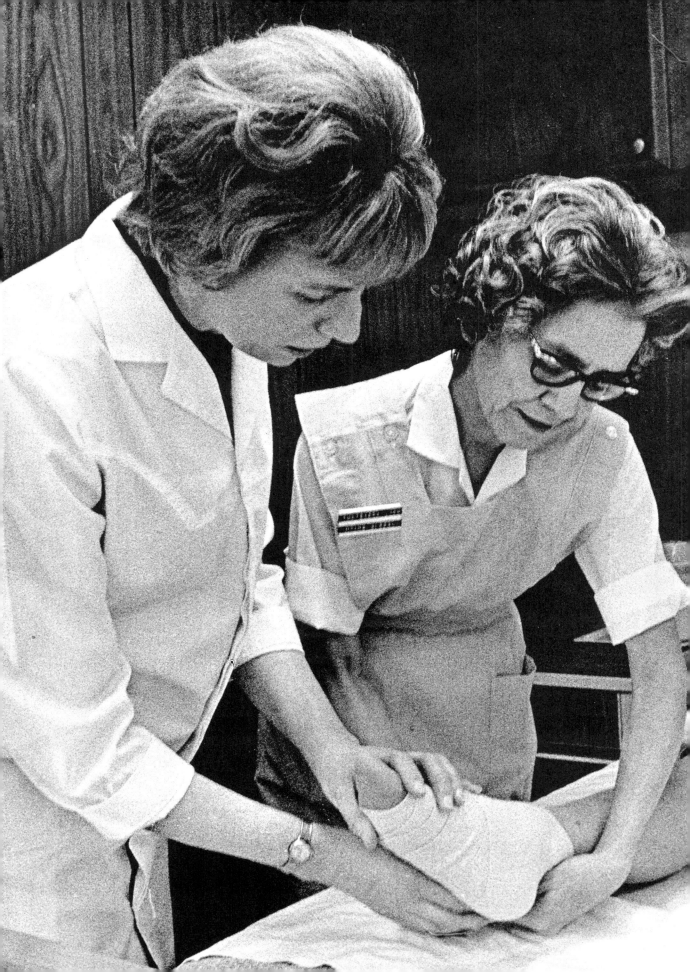

Twelfth Day

Doctors, Nurses, Chief Physician

Since my illness came shortly before the Christmas season, we were doubly blessed with letters of encouragement and hope. Among these I prize a number of letters from Christian doctors. One of these reads, "I hope that the doctors, through the wisdom and knowledge given from God, are being of real help to you. May His divine will be done, is our prayer." The writer of this prayer spent a period of years in Africa and India, alleviating suffering as she ministered to lepers, the tubercular, victims of malnutrition, and persons with disesaes we seldom see in our comfortable and privileged environment.

I have often wondered, as I wait in an immaculate and sterile doctor's office, what it would be like to live in an area of the world where one doctor serves many thousands of persons. Certainly, one would not run to a doctor with a scratch or a sore throat! And certainly, one would not expect to attain the proverbial threescore-years-and-ten.

And yet, in spite of sheets changed daily, good nursing care, and highly trained physicians, we easily become disgruntled. Why is that nurse so slow in bringing my pain pill? Does the doctor really have an interest in me personally?

Doctors and nurses vary in their degree of dedication, and compassion is more observable in some than in others. Because of a shortage of medical personnel, a patient has to learn to be "patient" in more ways than one. Often well-meaning but over-worked doctors and nurses are doing the best they can, but just cannot do all for us which we feel should be done.

There is one Physician, however, who is never hurried, never worried, and never too busy to hear our complaints. It is of this Physician that a friend writes, "I do hope and pray that you are getting the best of care . . . and that the doctors will have wisdom to know what to do for you . . . and above all that the Great Physician will help you to be healed completely, if that be His will."

39

Of this Great Healer of bodies and souls, Dr. Luke (a beloved physician himself) writes, "When the crowds learned it [where Jesus was], they followed him; and he welcomed them and spoke to them of the kingdom of God, and cured those who had need of healing" (Luke 9:11).

Peter Marshall, in a prayer for those who are sick, wrote:

"Lord Jesus, Thou art the Lord of lords, the King of kings. Thou art still the Ruler of this universe. Thou art its Great Architect.

"In the beginning, Thou didst design every part of it—from the twinkling of the great stars to the molding of the petals of the wayside flowers; from the coloring of the heavens to the tint of the butterflies' wings, even to this body of mine which is the temple of Thy Spirit. Hear me now as I pray for Thy healing touch.

"I confess that in my desperation and my need, I have wondered about the providence of God. Forgive, I pray, this lack of trust in His power and in His love.

"I acknowledge my unworthiness to ask Thee for any good gift. Yet I ask not on any merit of mine, but because of the claim purchased for me on the cross.

"Thou who didst Thyself explore all the vast treasures of pain on that cross, bestow upon me Thy grace.

"I have known Thee as the Saviour of my soul; now I would know Thee as the Saviour of my body. I would find in Thee this day the Great Physician."[1]

Word of Comfort:

Behold, the Lord's hand is not shortened,
    that it cannot save;
neither his ear heavy, that it cannot hear.

—Isaiah 59:1

1 From *The Prayers of Peter Marshall,* edited by Catherine Marshall. Copyright 1954 by Catherine Marshall. Used by permission of the publisher, McGraw-Hill Book Company. p. 55.

Thirteenth Day

"Before They Call I . . . Answer"

I can still remember the excitement of it. I was combing my hair in my third-class cabin room—somewhere in the middle of the Atlantic Ocean—when a steward knocked on the door to tell me that I had a telephone call on the first-class deck. In the next few moments I spoke by radio phone to my parents, hearing their voices for the first time in more than a year. Their voices were so clear and plain, that they might have been calling from another deck of the *Queen Mary*.

This is the kind of world we live in. A cancer patient in my hospital ward told me of a weekend she took off from her routine cobalt treatments to fly to Bermuda. "All my life I wanted to go to Bermuda, and now I had a little extra money," she said. Thus, this adventuresome patient boarded a jet all by herself and spent a weekend at a fancy hotel in the faraway island. Meeting her doctor in the selfsame hotel was a coincidence she had not anticipated!

We are only a few hours from any distant part of our world. We are only a few minutes from the voice of any of our friends. We are only a few days and a five-cent postage stamp from the wisdom and encouragement of any of our loved ones. And we are less than a second away from the help of God.

Prayer is a form of communication that knows no limits, either of time or space. It travels many light years in an instant. God has told us that He knows what we need, even before we ask Him. His ear is always tuned our way. He never sleeps. He never grows tired of our much speaking (although He may weary of our forgetting to talk with Him). He not only listens, but in His infinite power and love, He answers our call.

We thank God for our praying friends. They told of their prayers in many ways, bringing many pictures to my mind. "We think of you every day at family worship." I saw this devoted family, seated as olive plants around their fireplace, each one taking his turn in prayer. "We are constantly turning our thoughts toward you, and toward God *for* you." I could see this family praying as they went about their usual work. "Our people identify with you in concern," wrote a pastor. In their hearts these friends put themselves in our place. "I'll remember you daily." That was a promise, and I think she kept it. "Every morning (at a Christian publishing house) the prayer bell rings at eleven minutes before 10:00, we have silent prayer for one minute before coffee break. Be assured that each day at that time my prayers will ascend in your behalf." "We will stand by you in prayer." "We are constantly upholding you in prayer." "Your loved ones bear you up in prayer." Yes, we felt it.

But what was more exciting than an oceanic telephone call were four letters received after God had answered these prayers. Three different family friends wrote that for some reason God had laid our family on their hearts *before* they knew that an illness crisis had come to us. "I'm sure it was the Holy Spirit prompting me to offer up prayers on your behalf when we knew nothing of your hospitalization." This came from Indiana.

A second wrote, "Your letter has explained why we have often been led to pray for you folks." This came from British Columbia.

And a third read, "I can't explain it, but for several weeks before we received your letter you were brought to mind." This from Nebraska.

Then, immediately following a temporary setback, this note came from Pennsylvania: "I have been thinking of you so much the past several days. Have they been special days for you?"

There were letters from Brazil, Japan, and India—really only a prayer's breath away.

Let us not be too proud to ask for prayer. And let us spend some time, too, in talking to our Father about our friends who also need His love and help.

Word of Comfort:

Before they call, I will answer . . .
while they are yet speaking, I will hear.

—Isaiah 65:24

Fourteenth Day

"One Day at a Time"

I am thankful for authors who have pointed out Christ's sense of humor. When we read His words, as set down in the Bible, we have no way of knowing His tone of voice or the expression He had on His face. But there is good reason to believe that some things were said with a smile.

Take, for example, Jesus' words about tomorrow. He must have had at least a twinkle in His eye when He said, "So do not be anxious about tomorrow; tomorrow will look after itself. Each day has troubles enough of its own" (NEB).

That we are to live a day at a time is also brought out in the Lord's Prayer, where we are commanded to ask Him for our *daily* bread. I recently heard of some university students (fellows) who share an apartment. These boys decided to save a little time. When they do their weekly grocery shopping, they spread the supplies out on the kitchen table and thank God for all the meals of the coming week. That, it seems to me, is taking efficiency a bit too far!

A friend writes, "May you find your real peace and comfort in living in God's will a day at a time." Another puts it this way, "One thing is a great comfort, and that is that you will be given grace sufficient for each day."

Don't most of our anxieties come because we are not willing to live one day at a time? There is the past, often leering with its disheartening face. When we are ill, it seems that the wicked one takes advantage of our weakness to bring to mind things which God has already forgotten. The Apostle Paul wisely tells us, "Forgetting those things which are behind . . . I press toward the mark . . . of the high calling of God in Christ Jesus."

However, if we are reminded of sins of the past which we have not cleared from our consciences, God has the remedy for this. We can confess those sins and shortcomings and claim God's promise in I John 1:9: "If we confess our sins, he is faithful and just to forgive us our sins, and to cleanse us from all unrighteousness."

The future, too, may be particularly foreboding. Life is complicated enough, when we are well, when we are strong. How can we face the future with physical limitations? How serious is our illness? How will this or that affect our loved ones?

Again, we hear Christ's words: "How little faith you have! No, do not ask anxiously, 'What are we to eat? What are we to drink? What shall we wear?' . . . Your heavenly Father knows that you need them all. Set your mind on God's kingdom and his justice before everything else, and all the rest will come to you as well. . . . Do not be anxious about tomorrow" (NEB).

> He who hath led will lead
>   All through the wilderness,
> He who hath fed will surely feed. . . .
> He who hath blessed will bless:
> He who hath heard thy cry
>   Will never close His ear,
> He who hath marked thy faintest sigh
>   Will not forget thy tear.
> He loveth always, faileth never.
> So rest on Him today—forever.[1]

Word of Comfort:

And as your days, so shall your strength be.

         —Deuteronomy 33:25b

---

1. Frank Houghton, *Amy Carmichael of Dohnavur*. London SPCK. 1953. P. 46.

Fifteenth Day

"That I May Know How Frail I Am"

It struck me at first a little odd to comfort the sick with these words. Yet, the very words appeared in several letters, something to this effect: "Once again we are made to feel how frail and helpless we creatures are."

No one needed to tell me. "Would you mind jacking up my bed a bit?" "I'm sorry, but I can't reach my water." One day, trying to open a celluloid package of salad dressing, I had to ask for a clean gown; it had exploded all over me!

All our lives we hear admonitions on staying physically fit. Most of us who enjoy a fair measure of good health scarcely take time to think of the possibility of doing otherwise. That is, until a sudden turn of events lands us flat on our backs, dependent upon the good natures and services of others. I didn't particularly like to think of how frail I was, to tell the truth.

But one day I discovered that the psalmist asked God to show him his frailty. "Lord, make me to know mine end, and the measure of my days, what it is: that I may know *how frail I am*. Behold, thou hast made my days as an handbreadth; and mine age is nothing before thee: verily every man at his best state is altogether vanity."

In *The Seasons of Life*[1] Dr. Paul Tournier, a noted Christian psychiatrist, says, "Every sickness heralds the death which one day will come to put an end to our so fragile success." In other words, what the psalmist, as well as Dr. Tournier, is saying, is that we need to be reminded of the thin thread of life and the uncertainty of tomorrow. We need to remind ourselves that our lives are in God's hand.

The five young missionaries, who were martyred in Ecuador in 1956, felt that a missionary should consider his natural life as *expendable*. We know that our real personality, our spiritual self, is not that body which can be touched by danger, sickness, and death. Jesus told us not to be worried about what we eat or drink, nor about the body, what we wear, for our life itself is of more importance. He also said that we shouldn't fear those who

46

are able to kill the body, but that we should rather fear him who is able to destroy both soul and body.

It is true that while we are living in our frail bodies, we are all "of one piece." Our spiritual selves are often influenced by the state of our digestion or other discomforts. Yet God has promised that He will renew our inner person by His never-failing resources. "Though our outward man perish," Paul writes, "yet the inward man is renewed day by day."

Although we didn't ask for the experience of illness or disability, we find our attention taken from our self-satisfied activities and directed to Him who gave us our lives to enjoy, who placed us here for His purposes. The hymn writer puts it this way:

Frail children of dust, and feeble as frail,

In Thee do we trust, nor find Thee to fail;

Thy mercies how tender, how firm to the end!

Our Maker, Defender, Redeemer and Friend.

—From "Oh, Worship the King" by R. H. Grant

Word of Comfort:

He gives power to the faint; and to him who
has no might he increases strength.

—Isaiah 40:29

1. Paul Tournier, *The Seasons of Life*. John Knox Press, Richmond, Va. 1961. P. 46.

Sixteenth Day

His Presence—Our Peace

Whenever I sit down to write a note of sympathy or concern to someone else, I find myself praying that this person will realize how close God is and feel the presence of Jesus Christ. Many of my friends expressed this hope for me. And it is a good thought, for we know that God is near at hand, ready to hear us before we ever call. Many saints of the past have meditated upon "practicing the presence of God," becoming increasingly aware of His nearness.

Several years ago, a friend of mine, Catherine L———, wrote to me about her bout with pneumonia, and how she felt His presence in her hour of need.

"The first night in the hospital I was very weak and all lights were out already; in fact, I was just about asleep when the lung specialist came up the hall asking for me. He had just seen my X-rays, so he questioned me. And since I have had a weakness in my lungs since I was a baby, I was quite sure he must think I have lung cancer, even if he wouldn't say so. After a while he left, but I had much to think about and couldn't sleep, in spite of how tired I was. But just like that the Twenty-third Psalm ran through my mind, over and over. And I never experienced such meaning out of it before. No one came into my room, but it was as though someone put His arms around me and whispered peace to me (even if the doctor's verdict would be true). And I couldn't begin to explain the joy of feeling as if someone's arms were encircling me, yet no one was there visibly. But I know He was there. I often wondered how I'd react to such tragic news, and I suppose God saw fit to use this hospital stay to show me."

If Christ's presence is warm and assuring during life's difficult experiences, how much more will we depend upon Him when we make the transition into His presence forever. Another friend, Miriam Sieber Lind, writes of this in poetry form:

What did you do when the darkness fell
And you knew that your day was done?

I raised my eyes to the Hill—the Hills
Where they have no need of the sun.

And what, when the last face wavered and blurred
And you stood in the night alone?

A loved Voice whispered, whispered my name,
And a warm Hand covered my own.

And what, when you came to the dark stream's edge
In the wake of the death-bitter strife?

He carried me lovingly, lovingly through
And into the land of Life.[1]

Two friends once walked together down a lonely road, discussing the tragedy of their day. As they trudged along, a Stranger joined them and began asking questions. Soon this unknown Friend was explaining mysteries to them, speaking words of comfort. It was only after He broke bread with them at supper that the disciples recognized Christ, their Lord and Master, who had been with them all along.

Often we are unaware of His presence, yet He is here, waiting to bless and comfort us. "Behold, I stand at the door and knock," He says: "If any one hears my voice and opens the door, I will come in to him and eat with him, and he with me." It is we who must open the door.

Word of Comfort:

Come unto me, all ye that labour and are heavy laden,
   and I will give you rest.
Take my yoke upon you, and learn of me;
   for I am meek and lowly in heart:
   and ye shall find rest unto your souls.

                              —Matthew 11:28, 29

1. Miriam Sieber Lind, "What of the Night?" in *Such Thoughts of Thee.* Herald Press, Scottdale, Pa. 1952.

Seventeenth Day

Accept Life!

"In acceptance there is peace." So wrote an old friend, one who has tested this truth throughout a long and useful life. Another wrote, "I'm sure that you are constantly rejoicing in His ways of choosing for you. This brings contentment and rest to the soul."

Hard words, these! Although they sound good on paper. I must, as I muse upon them, remember other words from a wise and compassionate pastor. He said it, not in a preachy way, but in a musing sort of way, as though he had just repeated it to some-one else in the past few hours (perhaps to himself). "We must," he said gently, knowing that I was struggling with news of my illness, "learn to accept life."

But I thought that I had learned to accept this illness! That is, until a new rash of symptoms appeared. Then accepting seemed to start all over again!

I pause to think through what accepting life involves. Certainly, it includes life's limitations: illness, pain, frustration, disappointment, interruptions. We like our trains to arrive on schedule. We want our life to follow the plan we have made for ourselves. We don't enjoy interruptions, even in our reading, much less in our plans for the future. Yet, life presents circumstances which we need to accept!

And we must accept people, beginning with ourselves. If we paraphrase the Golden Rule thus, "Accept others as you accept yourself," we see that No. 1 is where we must begin. There are things about ourselves which we can change, mountains we can climb, horizons we can aim for, but we must at the same time accept the fact of our humanness, of our ofttimes failings, of our limitations. And this is true of our relationship with husbands, wives, children, parents, and friends. Everyone needs to feel accepted just as he is, and for what he is.

Catherine Marshall, in her book, *Beyond Ourselves*, says that acceptance of a situation in life is different for the Christian than a stoic resignation to "come what may." She tells of a letter which she received from Betty Elliot soon after Betty's missionary-husband's death at the hands of the savage Ecuador Aucas. Betty wrote, "Your solution to grief is just another way of giving the same answer that God gave me in the first empty days: Accept this. Only in acceptance lies peace—not in forgetting nor in resignation nor in busyness. His will is good and acceptable and perfect. . . ."

To this Catherine adds, "There is a difference between acceptance and resignation. One is positive; the other negative. Acceptance is creative, resignation sterile.

"Resignation is barren of faith in the love of God. It says, 'Grievous circumstances have come to me. There is no escaping them. I am only one creature, an alien in a vast unknowable creation. I have no heart left even to rebel. So I'll just resign myself to what apparently is the will of God; I'll even try to make a virtue out of patient submission.' So resignation lies down quietly in the dust of a universe from which God seems to have fled, and the door of hope swings shut.

"But turn the coin over. Acceptance says, 'I trust the good will, the love of my God. I'll open my arms and my understanding to what He has allowed to come to me. Since I know that He means to make all things work together for good, I consent to this present situation with hope for what the future will bring.' Thus acceptance leaves the door of hope wide open to God's creative plan."[1]

Let us remember that accepting life also includes accepting life's little joys, surprises, compensations, and opportunities for creative use of our setbacks. It is also accepting God's tremendous resources in difficult situations. Three times the Apostle Paul begged God to relieve him of some type of physical distress. But each time God, in His love, replied, "No, Paul, I have a purpose in permitting this inconvenience in your life at this time. My grace is sufficient for you, for my strength is made perfect in weakness."

Word of Comfort:

> For my thoughts are not your thoughts,
> neither are your ways my ways, says the Lord.
> For as the heavens are higher than the earth,
> so are my ways higher than your ways
> and my thoughts than your thoughts.
>
> —Isaiah 55:8, 9

1. From *Beyond Our Selves* by Catherine Marshall. Copyright © 1961 by Catherine Marshall. Used by permission of the publisher, McGraw-Hill Book Company, pp. 93, 94.

Eighteenth Day

Creative Troubles

A friend writes, "We take courage in your ability to see and utilize God's blessings in this experience."

Another says, "We are confident you have the resources to make it [your illness] a creative experience."

Blessings? A creative experience? I ponder this. I wish I were as confident as my friends. In a book on healing, the author asserts that God does not get much glory from our illnesses. She goes on to say that illness usually makes us quarrelsome, irritable, and peevish. She does admit, though, that there are examples of redemptive suffering.

It *is* hard to be patient when we are dependent upon others. Pain *can* cause us to be irritable and self-centered. We *do* have a tendency to look too much to ourselves and not enough to Christ. But God can come into the scene and sanctify even suffering to our spiritual growth. I think of the words of the hymn, "How Firm a Foundation," by George Keith which have often inspired me:

When through the deep waters I call thee to go,

The rivers of sorrow shall not overflow;

For I will be with thee thy troubles to bless,

And sanctify to thee thy deepest distress.

A minister, who was going through a difficult experience, discovered to his surprise that most of the New Testament was written in the context of suffering. When we think about it, how many of life's worthwhile lessons have been learned through the discipline and discoveries of the hard things of life? Would the hymns of Fanny Crosby, for instance, have been as rich and bountiful, had she had the gift of sight? Could most of our literature have been written in a vacuum, had not the authors experienced pain, suffering, disappointment, tragedy? Could any of us truly comfort another, had we never experienced the need for comfort ourselves? Could we rejoice with those who do rejoice, if we did not know joy in our own lives? Could we weep with those who weep, had we never known sorrow?

It is in times of distress that we realize the love of our friends, when they say things like this to us: "Words can't express my feeling of sympathy to you. . . . We shed real tears with you. . . . Our hearts go out to you."

Sometime ago we visited friends whose teenage son had suddenly been sent to the hospital with a severe case of diabetes. Now this family has a pleasant habit of making homemade ice cream once a week. As we sat around the table enjoying the usual treat, Bob, the father, tried to swallow a lump in his throat as he said, "You know, if Dave can't enjoy this ice cream anymore, then it doesn't taste good to me, either."

Not only do we learn anew the love of friends and family when difficulties come, but we are reminded of the love of the heavenly Father. With time to meditate on His goodness, we learn to abandon our personal plans and ambitions, our self-sufficiency and our pride, and our own feeble struggles to the almighty and all-powerful hand of God.

God, Thou art love! I build my faith on that. . . .
I know Thee who has kept my path and made
Light for me in darkness, tempering sorrow
So that it reached me like solemn joy.
It were too strange that I should doubt
   Thy love.

—Browning

Word of Comfort:

It is good for me that I was afflicted,
that I might learn thy statutes.

—Psalm 119:71

Nineteenth Day

Why?

A missionary friend told me that she once had a maid who drove her almost to distraction. Each time she assigned the woman a task, she was asked, "Why? Why should I do it this way, or why should I do it at all?" Now there is a stage in the development of our small child when we expect to hear the question, "Why?" A friend once wrote to me: "Wait till you have a smart, restless five-year-old who should be in school, then you'll know what it's like to hear, 'What does this word say? Which day of the week is this? What time is it? How do you make a Q? What comes after 29? How do they make shoe polish? Why do you sing so loud? Why is Jamie a boy?'"

But the question, "Why?" which comes to us during hard experiences is different from the "why" of a small child or the "why" of the exasperating maid. This "why" is a deep and nagging threat to our peace of mind. It can form itself into a doubt—a doubt as to the existence and love of God or a doubt as to our own integrity and worthiness as a child of His. Perhaps that is the reason so many of my friends wrote me saying not to ask the question, Why? Here are some of their words of counsel:

"It is not easy for us to know and understand why God allows us to go through these dark experiences, but there is a joy and comfort to know—He is near and will go with us. . . ."

"We dare not question, 'Why?' when trials come, but seek the blessing our Lord has designed in allowing these testings."

"We do not know why some Christians are faced with certain problems. As M——— once said, 'A Christian should not ask *why*, but *how* can I witness through this experience.'"

"A person can ask so many questions when something like this enters our lives, but I guess we must be content not to know all the answers but lean upon Christ, knowing that His way is the best way."

From other comforting friends came these significant statements:

"It must be hard at times to remember that God's purposes are fulfilled in long-range plans that seem to have difficult intervals in them."

57

"God is surely leading and preparing you for greater service."

"I have so often failed to see His hand. . . ."

"We see only the under side of God's working; the top side has the more distinct pattern."

The thought of God's overall design for our life struck a familiar note, and sometime later I ran across this poem:

LIFE

The Heavenly Weaver deftly weaves
  Upon His loom each day.
The pattern of our lives takes form
  In an often puzzling way:
Dark threads and light are intertwined
  In ways that seem unwise;
But when it's done, a masterpiece
  Unfolds before our eyes!

Word of Comfort:

And we know that all things work together for good to them that love God, to them who are called according to his purpose.

—Romans 8:28

Twentieth Day

Consecrated Talents

Many voices spoke to me during my convalescence—voices from the past, voices of new friends, voices of medical authority, and voices of people I did not know. One such was a radio announcer who said, in effect, "We must not stress the *disability* of a person, but emphasize his *abilities.*" He was pleading for employment for the handicapped. As I thought of these words, however, it seemed that they applied to anyone, for have we not all some kind of handicap to overcome?

It is not only during times of illness or disability that one struggles with a sense of one's worth. All of us hold a mental image of ourselves as whole persons, functioning in our world with efficiency and dispatch. Thus, an older person who can no longer scrub floors and make garden may be tempted to feel that he is no longer of much value, forgetting the contribution of his very presence to his friends, children, and grandchildren. A new mother often feels frustrated because of her limited strength and inability to perform routine tasks as she did before the baby's birth. A father, temporarily out of work, may feel loss of self-respect as he struggles over the family budget.

In every situation where life seems to "clip our wings," we must remember what the announcer said about the handicapped. We must minimize our disabilities and ask God how we can most creatively use the abilities which He has given us.

Jesus told the story of three men, each of whom was presented with some money to be invested for his employer. The man who received the largest amount faithfully invested his five talents and received five talents as profit. The servant who received the two talents did the same, earning two more. But the last servant, poor fellow, felt handicapped because he was given only one talent to invest. Taking this money out into the garden, he dug a hole and buried it. When his employer returned, it was still in the ground, rotting away. And because he was such a poor steward of his one talent, even this was taken away from him.

Our health, the use of our hands, our eyes, our feet, our mind, are all talents which God has bestowed upon us. He has left none of us without some ability which we can use for Him, even in weakness. As I write this, I admire a Christmas greeting which came during the past month. The painting on the cover is called "The Carolleers," and the information on the card says that it was done in 1840 with the mouth of I. Schricker. This man apparently had no use of his hands, but succeeded in creating a better oil painting than most of us could have done with all our faculties.

A few years ago a young surgeon, Dr. Mary Verghese, took a holiday from her work at the Christian Medical College at Vellore, India. But the outing proved to be a tragedy, almost unexplainable in human terms. The automobile in which she was traveling rolled over a bank, throwing Mary to the ground and making her a paraplegic for life.

After much suffering and adjusting to her new situation, Mary thought one day of the words of the hymn, "Take My Life," by Frances R. Havergal:

> Take my life, and let it be
> Consecrated, Lord, to Thee:
> Take my hands and let them move
> At the impulse of Thy love. . . .

She still had her hands! And they were skilled in performing delicate surgery, in bringing new hope to leprosy patients who had lost the use of their hands and who were disfigured by ugly scars. Today, as a result of fresh insights and training, Dr. Mary Verghese heads a new department of Physical Medicine and Rehabilitation. She says, "Without the accident, I might have been only an ordinary doctor. Now I have been shown the way to help patients whose needs, in India, were unmet before." Her story is told in a book, *Take My Hands*,[1] and is an inspiration to any of us to make the best use of the talents God has given us.

Two glad services are ours,
Both the Master loves to bless.
First we serve with all our powers—
Then with all our feebleness.

Nothing else the soul uplifts
Save to serve Him night and day,
Serve Him when He gives His gifts—
Serve Him when He takes away.

—C. A. Fox

Word of Comfort:

I can do all things in him who strengthens me.
—Philippians 4:13

1. Dorothy Clarke Wilson, *Take My Hands.* McGraw-Hill Book Company, Inc., New York. 1963.

Twenty-first Day

A Vessel for Honor

"God must have a special love for you and your family, to call you to experience this trial. Just remember He is doing this for His *glory*." This thought, penned on the back of a Christmas greeting which began, "Glory to God," was not a new idea. Others had reminded me that illness can be a glory to God. The psalmist himself said something like that: "Call upon me in the day of trouble: I will deliver thee, and thou shalt glorify me."

But how can one glorify Christ by being sick? Certainly not by trying! Sometimes it seems that the harder we *try* to glorify God, the more likely we are to end up glorifying ourselves!

Then one day I received a letter which took me back to a sacred hour in a little farm home in Markham, Ontario. My husband and I had been serving in a conference in this community. Although we had never met the Russell Groves, we had heard of their son, who glorified God in his death. For one day, as this young missionary was registering students for school in Somalia, a maddened religious fanatic suddenly came up behind him, stabbed him and his wife, Dorothy, and left them to die. Merlin's wife recovered from her wounds, but his body lies in a simple grave in the country to which he was called.

In the hour which we spent in the Grove home, we looked through photograph albums showing the childhood and youth of this dedicated young man, we listened to the story of his parents' visit to his field of labor before his death, and heard of the work which he had begun in Somalia. And we heard how his death as a martyr had, as usually happens, only furthered the cause of Christ. For his parents, there was neither bitterness nor rebellion, only loving memories and a desire to continue the work which their son had left unfinished.

Now Mrs. Grove wrote, "I wrote to Jim Elliot's[1] mother . . . and at Christmastime she sent a card and a note which blessed my soul. I want to pass some of it on to you. . . . She called me Sister Grove, although we are strangers, and said having experienced the same sorrow, makes us closer in His fellowship. She [Mrs.

Elliot] writes, 'I'm in my fourth week of complete bed rest because of a recurrent osteomyelitis, trying to avoid another surgery—one more of God's ordered experiences to make the clay pliable for shaping a vessel to honor.' "

Clay in the hands of the potter! Perhaps some of us have watched a potter work, or have dabbled in ceramics ourselves. Now I remember Hannah Whitall Smith's use of this illustration in her book, *The Christian's Secret of a Happy Life*.[2] She says, "The lump of clay could never grow into a beautiful vessel if it stayed in the clay pit for thousands of years; but when it is put into the hands of a skillful potter it grows rapidly, under his fashioning, into the vessel he intends it to be. And in the same way the soul, abandoned to the working of the Heavenly Potter, is made into a vessel unto honor . . . for the Master's use."

My part, then, is simply to place my life, hopes, ambitions, joys, troubles, fears, frustrations, my past, present, and future into the hands of the One whose love for me has been proved over and again. He, the Potter, will make the clay of my life into a useful vase, a work which does credit to the artist who planned it.

Long is the way, and very steep the slope,
Strengthen me once again, O God of Hope.

Far, very far, the summit doth appear;
But Thou art near, my God, but Thou art near.

And Thou wilt give me with my daily food,
Powers of endurance, courage, fortitude.

Thy way is perfect; only let that way
Be clear before my feet from day to day.

Thou art my Portion, saith my soul to Thee,
O what a Portion is my God to me.

—Amy Carmichael

Word of Comfort:

But now, O Lord, thou art our father;
we are the clay, and thou our potter;
and we all are the work of thy hand.

—Isaiah 64:8

1. One of the five martyred missionaries, whose story is told in *Shadow of the Almighty* and *Through Gates of Splendor*, both by Elisabeth Elliot.

2. Hannah Whitall Smith, *The Christian's Secret of a Happy Life*, Fleming H. Revell Co., Westwood, N.J. 1952. P. 32.

Twenty-second Day

"Who Healeth . . . Thy Diseases"

It was just a short note from a minister-uncle. "So sorry to learn of your illness," he penned, "but hope it will be pleasing to our Lord to touch your body with healing, all to His glory. I know many are remembering you in their prayers."

Healing? Yes, I knew that right now, right at this moment, Christ, the Great Physician, could touch my body and heal me completely. There had been healings in my family. There was, for instance, my Grandmother, whose head, face, and neck had been involved with erysipelas, which would have been fatal had it gone further. Grandfather, too, had the disease, and Grandma had been taking care of him (all this happened during the worst of the Depression). In simple faith, Grandma talked matters over with the Lord. She told Him that she didn't know what would happen if she, too, became sick, that there just was no one available to take care of both her and Papa. Then she went to bed and fell asleep. From the next morning on, she continued to improve until she was completely well. And Grandpa, too, recovered.

Our baby daughter was weak and emaciated by a severe case of diarrhea. When a group of Christian musicians came to our church for a conference on church music, Becky was ready for hospitalization. In earnest prayer, these friends lifted our Becky to God. From that hour she improved at an amazing speed!

All healing is a miracle; all healing is from God. But not always does God bring immediate, on-the-spot recovery. Sometimes He heals by natural means, through doctors and nurses who use their training, skills, and drugs to alleviate suffering. Sometimes God's love must be channeled through a human instrument to one who is suffering from lack of love. Sometimes God uses time, work, music, and hobbies to heal one who is suffering from nervous exhaustion. And sometimes God touches the human body with instantaneous supernatural healing.

A minister's wife, who for many years has served the church in a foreign land and in women's work in the Midwest, tells of an experience which she had in high school.

"While playing basketball I fell, injuring my knee. It ended in a bad case of tetanus. My life was despaired of for a number of days. My one leg had become black and blue like a log. They had given more serum than was thought possible. The doctor considered amputation. My friends and teachers were much in prayer. My mother had come to be with me. One night, as she was half asleep on her bed, she heard a voice say to her, 'Saved to serve.' From that time she had full faith I would get well. . . ." And she did!

However, she goes on to say, "It is my conviction that all prayers must be prayed within the will of God. He works in our hearts. Sickness can be so valuable when it is permitted to touch our spirits in such a way as to draw us closer in His love. It isn't so significant that I live ten more years than I would otherwise, but that my sickness contribute to my spiritual life and bring living faith and blessing to others—that *is* significant."

In the Bible we have examples of all kinds of healing. God told Hezekiah to use a lump of figs for his boil. Timothy was urged to drink a little wine for his stomach's sake. The Good Samaritan, with t.l.c. (tender loving care), poured oil on the wounds of his friend. Paul took Dr. Luke along on his journeys. God expects us to use natural means of healing.

Jesus, on the other hand, healed many diseases outright, as He preached the kingdom of God. More important, He forgave sins and healed the minds and spirits of those who suffered. His heart of compassion went out to all who were in pain and trouble.

And then we have in the Bible examples of people who were not healed physically, but who lived victoriously within the framework of their difficulty. To Paul, who had some unexplained thorn-in-the-flesh, God's answer came, "My grace is sufficient for thee."

Whether God's will is to heal us immediately or gradually, or to give us grace to live with our problem, we know that He wills all of us to be whole in spirit and in soul. Let us ask Him to touch our lives, the real us, with His healing hand, taking from us all barriers to His perfect will, all resentments, grudges, ill will, fears, worries, and guilt. And then let us place our lives in the hand of One who has our best interests at heart, who sees our lives in the light of His eternity. We can trust that hand.

Word of Comfort:

Bless the Lord, O my soul,
and forget not all his benefits,
who forgives all your iniquity,
who heals all your diseases,
who redeems your life from the Pit,
who crowns you with steadfast love and mercy,
who satisfies you with good as long as you live so that your youth
is renewed like the eagle's.

—Psalm 103:2-5

Twenty-third Day

Profiles in Courage

If there was one word which "bugged" me during my illness, it was the word "courage." Everywhere I turned, I faced it. Sometimes my friends told me I had it. Sometimes I told them I didn't. Many of my "comforters" wrote me that they prayed that I would possess this elusive virtue. Or they prayed that it had already been granted me. I read articles on courage, which still left me in the dark as to what it really is.

One book, which I can recommend to those who are experiencing difficulty, *The Storm and the Rainbow,* by Lowell Russell Ditzen, describes courage thus, giving credit to Robert Frost for some of these ideas:

"Courage is the capacity to go ahead, it is the will to act on limited knowledge . . . it is marked by an attempt to make the best of any situation without whining. . . . The courage that we exhibit reaches out to touch others; it is passed on, it spreads out, giving courage to other men who may only need our example to find their own source of strength."[1]

And then there is the source of all good definitions, the dictionary. Courage, says Webster, is "that quality of mind which enables one to meet danger and difficulties with firmness; valor."

Obviously, we never need to develop courage unless we have obstacles and difficulties; the very word implies that there are dangers and troubles. The late President John F. Kennedy has immortalized a number of men of courage in his book, *Profiles in Courage.*[2] These stories tell of persons who stood alone for principle to create equality and liberty for all, to make for peace, to lead the nation in right paths. But their decisions were costly. Some lost their reputation, their position, their lives, and their honor for the unpopular course which they knew to be right. They were subjected to ridicule, criticism, and intense personal suffering. Of them the late president, himself a profile in courage, says, "The stories of past courage can . . . teach, they can offer hope, they can provide inspiration. But they cannot supply courage itself. For this each man must look into his own soul."

Soon after World War II my husband and I worked with refugees who had fled into western Germany from behind the Iron Curtain. We shall never forget the faith and courage of most of our refugee friends, in spite of painful memories of separation from loved ones, violence, and death. Yet there were those who had, as the Apostle Paul puts it, allowed a "root of bitterness" to spring up within them, choking out the inner resources of faith and confidence in God's love.

A friend, who has faced illness and handicap with courage, shared with me this poem-prayer:

God make me brave for life,
Oh, braver than this!
Let me straighten after pain,
As a tree straightens after rain
Shining and lovely again.

God make me brave for life,
Much braver than this!
As the blown grass lifts let me rise
From sorrow with quiet eyes,
Knowing Thy way is wise.

God make me brave—Life brings
Such blinding things.
Help me to keep my sight,
Help me to see aright
That out of the dark—comes light.

Word of Comfort:

Be strong and of good courage;
be not frightened, neither be dismayed;
for the Lord your God is with you
wherever you go.

—Joshua 1:9

1. Lowell Russell Ditzen, *The Storm and the Rainbow.* Henry Holt and Co., New York. 1959. Pp. 17, 18.
2. John F. Kennedy, *Profiles in Courage,* Harper and Brothers, New York. 1955. P. 246.

Twenty-fourth Day

"Thy Going Out . . . Thy Coming In"

"I will restore health unto thee, and I will heal thee of thy wounds, saith the Lord." This little excerpt from Jeremiah appeared on a homemade card from a near-relative. I believed that God could heal me, but I was impatient, as I lay in the hospital, watching nurses hurry up and down the halls on their two good legs. Did they properly appreciate their legs? Often I had the urge to get out of bed and go over to comfort a fellow patient. But my limbs were not functioning.

In the climax of my discouragement one day, a greeting came to me from friends of my parents, an old couple whom I have seen perhaps once in my lifetime. In their note God had inspired these friends to remind me of another verse, which answered my special need of the moment. I took this verse as God's voice for the day. "Wait on the Lord: be of good courage, and he shall strengthen thine heart."

Wait! I never liked waiting. Patience is not one of my virtues. Waiting is not my "cup of tea." Of course, God could have healed me spontaneously, when I first came to Him with the request, or when friends gathered to pray as I was anointed with oil by my pastor. The service had been meaningful and had supplied strength and courage. But an immediate healing was not God's plan for me. And I would not question His wisdom.

What bothered me more than the weakness in my legs was the loss of the use of my right hand and the partial use of the left. It is humiliating for an adult to have to ask another to comb her hair. How I hated to call an aide to pick up a book which had clumsily fallen from my hand! Of what possible worth would I be as a mother, if I could not use my hands? Did those nurses appreciate their fingers, which moved with such flexibility and speed at their command? Probably not.

Each night, as lights finally went off in our ward, I would ask Christ to come into our room and watch over us, giving us a sense of His presence. One night I had a dream, not the ordinary variety which is quickly forgotten, but a special dream, vivid and real. I dreamed that when I returned home, I found that my fingers functioned again, and that I could type rapidly on our electric typewriter. Because the dream seemed so real, I told it to my doctor in the morning. He only smiled and said, "I wish we could make dreams come true."

In my case God had led us through a series of providential circumstances to a medical center where a drug was being used experimentally to help some patients with multiple sclerosis. God seemingly used this drug to bring strength back to my legs and to give me eventual use of my fingers. Although I am not cured, the dream of typing did come true, and as a result I am able to write this book. At the moment of this writing, I am walking, a real adventure when one has to learn all over again with the help of balance bars, crutches, and canes.

Hitherto hath the Lord helped [*me*]. He has not promised a glimpse into the future, but has given strength for the day, grace sufficient for every period of testing as it comes. And this is all He promises anyone, sick or well. As I thank Him for the ability to walk out my front door, I think of another verse sent to me by one of "my comforters." Perhaps it will also serve as a *Word of Comfort* for you.

The Lord shall preserve thy going out
   and thy coming in
   from this time forth,
   and even for evermore.

          Amen.

God moves in a mysterious way,
His wonders to perform;
He plants His footsteps in the sea,
And rides upon the storm.

Ye fearful saints, fresh courage take;
The clouds ye so much dread
Are big with mercy, and shall break
In blessings on your head.

Judge not the Lord by feeble sense,
But trust Him for His grace;
Behind a frowning providence
He hides a smiling face.

His purposes will ripen fast,
Unfolding ev'ry hour;
The bud may have a bitter taste,
But sweet will be the flow'r.

Blind unbelief is sure to err,
And scan His work in vain;
God is His own interpreter,
And He will make it plain.

—William Cowper

The Author

Born in Harrisonburg, Virginia, Helen Good Brenneman spent her childhood years near Hyattsville, Maryland, a suburb of Washington, D.C. She studied at Eastern Mennonite and Goshen colleges, and worked for four years as a clerk in the U.S. Department of Agriculture. Always interested in writing, Helen longed as a girl to become a newspaper reporter, but later found herself instead writing articles, stories, women's inspirational talks, and devotional books.

Following her marriage to Virgil Brenneman in 1947, the couple served a year in a refugee camp operated by the Mennonite Central Committee in Gronau, Germany, before going to Goshen, Indiana, where her husband studied for the ministry. They served for ten years in two pastorates, at Iowa City, Iowa, and Goshen, Indiana. At the present time Mr. Brenneman is Executive Secretary of the campus ministries of the Mennonite Church. The Brennemans are the parents of two boys and two girls, at home, as well as a foster daughter, Mrs. Jack Birky, of Eugene, Oregon.

In 1964 the family spent a year in Boston, where Mr. Brenneman studied under a Danforth Foundation Grant. It was during this year that Helen became disabled and hospitalized with multiple sclerosis. And it was at this time that her "comforters" came to the fore with inspiration which she felt she must share with others going through similar crises. Thus she wrote *My Comforters.*

Other books by Mrs. Brenneman are *But Not Forsaken, Meditations for the New Mother,* and the January section of *Breaking Bread Together,* edited by Elaine Sommers Rich.

CREDITS
Edward Wallowitch, 10, 21, 48, 49, 59, 70, 71
H. Armstrong Roberts, 15
Grant Heilman, 16
Paul M. Schrock, 26, 32, 45
Rohn Engh, 38
Alan Cliburn, 52
Three Lions, 60
Eva Luoma, 64
C. Richard Krall, 74
Kermit Lind, 78
Joseph Alderfer, Book Design